Archie's Awful Apples

Making Alliteration Fun For All Types!

ISBN: 978-1-964411-00-2 (Paperback)

Any references to historical events, real people, or real places are used fictitiously. Names, characters, and places are products of the author's imagination.

Front cover image and book design by Amber Leigh Luecke

Printed in the United States of America

First printing edition 2024

Dedicated to all of the great teachers
who believe in their students.

Archie has an apple tree, but there is a problem...

When Archie eats one of the apples,
there is an awkward ant inside!

Archie screams and drops the apple. It is not an amazing apple after all! The awkward ant looks at Archie and says, "I live in that awful apple!"

Archie does not approve of the ant in his apple! He crosses his arms. "You must not live in my apples," he says. "Live in the almond tree across the field!"
"I do not like almonds," says the ant. "I love my awful apple. It is perfect for me!"

Archie is angry. He wants the ant to go away. He stomps inside his apartment and comes back out with an axe. Angry Archie wants to use the ax to chop down the apple tree with the ant inside!

Archie swings his ax, and the ant yells,
"Stop! I will bring my army of ants to
eat your apples if you don't go away!"
"These are my apples," says Archie.
"I will not argue."

"Please! I have a baby."

The ant shows Archie his ant baby.

"An ant baby!" Archie lowers his ax.

"I thought you were alone! Are there

other ants in my apple tree?"

"My aunt, the ant, lives in the apples as

well!"

The aunt steps out of the apple and crosses her arms. "I love this apple tree and all these apples," the ant aunt says. "Do not argue with us. We can live together!"

15

Archie looks up and sees all the ants on all the apples. "How do you like it up there?" Archie asks. Another ant answers Archie.

"It is very airy up here in the apples!" Archie realized the ants were right.

Angry Archie was not angry anymore. The awkward ant climbs up Archie's ankle and asks him again, "Can we please stay in your apple tree? It is the only home we have. If you chop down the tree, then no one will have apples!"

"You are allowed to stay in the apple tree," says Archie. "It is all of ours."

Now, the ants live in the apple tree high in the air and are allowed to stay as long as they want.

Discover the Wonders of Alliteration:
A Complete Collection from A to Z!

Dive into a world of wonder and learning with the "Alliteration Fun for All Types" Complete Collection, where each amusing story is dedicated to a specific letter of the alphabet.

From adventurous ants to zany zebras, these captivating tales are designed to engage and empower readers of all types, including those with dyslexia or other learning differences.

This collection of fun stories weaves rhythm, rhyming, and the magic of alliteration to foster a love of reading and promote inclusivity in storytelling.

Whether you're seeking an educational adventure, or inspiring a new reader, this collection promises to captivate young minds and instill a lifelong love for the magic of words.

To learn more visit Nickysbooks.com

amazon
⭐⭐⭐⭐⭐

If you enjoyed this book, please leave a review on Amazon and help new readers discover Nicky's books.
Thank you.

www.ingramcontent.com/pod-product-compliance
Lightning Source LLC
Chambersburg PA
CBHW041447120626
46547CB00002B/379